ESCAPING
THE
STORM

HOW TO DISCOVER
TRUE HAPPINESS
AND WORTH

KIM FORD

Dear Janette—
How can I ever thank you
for all your help? Your gifts have made
the process of me finding my truth & the
real me possible. That is an amazing
ability! I am so grateful for your
friendship & love. You are a gift from God!
—I ♡ ya! Kim Ford

ISBN-13 978-1539337478

Library of Congress Control Number: 2016916975
Published by CreateSpace Independent Publishing Platform,
North Charleston, SC

Author image by Livia Pewtress, www.LiviaDesigns.com

Information about hurricanes used from
earthobservatory.nasa.gov/Features/Hurricanes/Archive/original.pdf

To my husband. Thanks for never giving up on me.

LOST

The girl I once was is gone.
I'm lost, afraid, confused.
Where is she?
It seems so long ago I embraced her
And loved her
But somehow, somewhere
She disappeared
My heart aches.
I long to hear her laughter
To feel her joys
Carefree. Fun.
I wonder if she'll ever return?
I stumble around in darkness.
She must return!
I can't live without her
Scared, alone, lost
My head constantly spinning
Feeling nothing
Void.
Please help me find that little girl.

Lost
By: Kim Ford

June 3, 2001

It's 11:00 PM. I have so much going on in my head right now. I don't know how to begin, so I'm just going to list and brainstorm what I am feeling and thinking. I feel small, tired, vulnerable, weak, scared, confused, alone, unsupported, tension, pain, and a strong desire to quit.

Sometimes I feel like I need a vacation. Sometimes I want to be a child again so I could curl up in my mother's arms. To feel safe, to know everything is being taken care of, and that everything will be okay.

I'm tired and exhausted by responsibility. Every day it's the same thing. I've felt monotony before, but trying to deal with it in an everyday routine and the monotony of fighting or dealing with this depression is more than I can stand at times. There is a constant battle going on inside me. Always wondering what I need to do to find myself and fighting with all my might to keep holding on.

I'm so tired. I want to rest...completely rest. But, the battle continues. It never lets up. It makes me wonder, will it ever end? More importantly, how will it end? That's the part that scares me the most.

INTRODUCTION

FOR ALMOST FOUR YEARS, I LIVED IN PALM BAY, FLORIDA, WHERE I was introduced to hurricanes. I learned about hurricane seasons, the preparation necessary when they are headed your way, the concerns and dangers that start before hurricanes even hit land, and the damage and cleanup required after they pass. Hurricanes are known as the greatest storms on earth. This book is about my own personal hurricane named Depression, and how I escaped from its clutches. Hurricanes are destructive, frightening, and chaotic, so what better representation of our own personal life storms than a hurricane? As I experienced my own personal hurricane, I definitely felt like I was in the middle of the greatest storm on earth!

In this book, you will learn how to discover what "stage of the storm" you are currently experiencing. You will learn that escape from this turmoil is most definitely possible. You will understand how to be prepared for future storms and possibly how to avoid some altogether. As you learn how to conquer the personal hurricane that is wreaking havoc on you at this time, you will gain a better understanding of true happiness and how to obtain actual joy. You will also discover the great love your Savior has for you personally. As a result, your individual worth will increase and you will understand there is a purpose for your existence right now!

Everyone experiences personal storms, but we have a choice to decide if we are going to remain in those storms forever, or set ourselves free with Christ's help. It took me over sixteen years to understand escape was possible. My hope for you is that through my story, you will be set free from the chaos of your own storm sooner than I was. The choice of freedom is yours. If you continue reading this book, be prepared to see the real and raw side of me. I am including personal journal entries during the darkest parts of my journey through this storm. These journal entries are not in chronological order, but best describe my state of mind at particular stages of my specific storm. Please be respectful and kind as you read these accounts; it's not an easy thing for me to be so vulnerable.

At the end of most chapters in this book, there will be an opportunity for you to participate in an exercise or challenge. Please be prepared to do some brainstorming (no pun intended). I love to brainstorm! Writing freely without serious thought is one of the most freeing and helpful ways of getting what's in your mind and heart on paper in order to see it clearly. I personally enjoy brainstorming in bullet point or list fashion with my colorful Sharpies. There is no right or wrong way to brainstorm, just do it. I encourage you to participate in these exercises. Ask God for help as you think about, write, and accept the challenges given in this book. If you choose to participate wholeheartedly, your eyes will be opened to how much God loves you and how much His hand is a part of your life. It's not always easy to see God's love for us. Be patient in the process of receiving insight and understanding your worth in God's eyes. Recognizing and believing you are loved unconditionally is SO worth it!

I don't know you personally, but I love you nonetheless. Please understand that the journal entries and my personal experience may be very different than your own, but the lessons I have learned though escaping my storm can be applied to anyone struggling with their own personal storm. A storm is a storm no matter your age, situation, or gender. I know the feelings you are experiencing as your storm threatens to destroy you. I know the feelings of fear, hopelessness, worthlessness, despair, darkness, confusion, pain, sorrow, depression, and much, much more because I have lived with them. Please let me share what has helped me escape my greatest storm.

PART 1

IN THE BEGINNING

CHAPTER 1

FAVORABLE CONDITIONS

Master, the tempest is raging!
The billows are tossing high!
The sky is o'ershadowed with blackness.
No shelter or help is nigh.
Carest thou not that we perish?
How canst thou lie asleep
When each moment so madly is threat'ning
A grave in the angry deep?

(*Hymns*. "Master, the Tempest Is Raging," 105, vs. 1.
Words by Mary Ann Baker, music by H.R. Palmer)

IT WAS MY SENIOR YEAR IN HIGH SCHOOL. I WAS IN CONCERT CHOIR, and on this particular day we had a special guest coming to teach us how to sing "gospel singing" style. In preparation for our visitor, we as a choir had learned the song,

"Master, the Tempest is Raging". I had always loved this particular hymn, but I loved it even more after learning how to sing it in gospel singer fashion!

Our choir began singing; "Master, the tempest is raging! The billows are tossing high! The sky is o'er-shadowed with blackness. No shelter or help is nigh." We clapped along while swaying side to side, "Carest thou not that we perish? How canst thou lie asleep when each moment so madly is threat'ning, a grave in the angry deep?" I was in love with gospel style singing! I was having so much fun! Why didn't we sing like this at church? Little did I know as a high school student, singing a favorite hymn in a new favorite way, that I would be experiencing a storm like none other in a matter of just a few years.

Growing up, I had a great home life. I was fortunate to have amazing friends all through my school years. I lived in a safe neighborhood from the time I was born until the time I got married and moved out. Most importantly, I grew up loving God and I knew He loved me.

When I graduated from high school, I had so many dreams that I wanted to experience. My dreams included traveling the world, exploring different cultures, graduating from college, and having one great adventure after another. However, God had other plans for me. After attending a year of college, I met my future husband and within a very short amount of time, we were married. Two years later, we had our first child. I loved spending my days with our baby and was grateful I didn't have to work outside our home. Life was great. I do admit that as my friends' college graduation announcements arrived in the mail, I felt a tinge of jealousy, but I knew God had put me on this path for a reason, even if I didn't fully understand it. Life continued to go well. Of course we had our occasional ups and downs, but all in all, family life was good.

After my husband graduated from college, we moved to Florida. I was so excited to spread my wings! This was my chance to live somewhere else and meet tons of new people. The street we lived on had several different nationalities and I was in heaven with all the diversity and what I could learn from my new neighbors! Almost two years later, our next child was born. We were very busy serving in our church while living in Florida, but I loved the people, sunshine, beaches, and the fact that there was no snow! Without going into great detail, the birth of our second child was a bit traumatic, so when I felt God was prompting us to have another baby eight months later, I was quite resistant. However, after much prayer, my husband and I decided to do what God was asking us to do and started planning for another child.

When a hurricane is about to form, there are many factors that go into play. If the weather provides "favorable conditions," hurricanes begin to form from tropical disturbances as the surface pressure begins to fall in the area around the storm. The first signs of these disturbances are thunderstorms.

At this particular time in my life, I was unaware that just beyond the horizon, personal thunderstorms were forming, the pressure was beginning to drop, and the greatest storm of my life was about to smack me right in the face.

CHAPTER 2

THE SIGNS

September 12, 2000

I'm having a relapse of the horrible day I had Sunday. I managed to stay nice, but I feel like I am teetering on the edge of a nervous breakdown. Why am I having such a hard time coping with people, life, everything?! What do I do? I've delegated as much as I feel I can. I'm trying to limit my activities, but nothing seems to work. Help! All I want to do is exist with my little family; nothing more. That in itself overwhelms me, but I feel I could handle it. However, when you add everything else, even doing things I use to enjoy with my friends, it sets me into a state of panic. I just want to be left alone.

HERE WERE MY FIRST SIGNS OF WHAT MY STORM WAS GOING TO look like. I truly felt like I was losing my mind and it scared me. Everything I had done in the past to get out of situations where I felt sad were not working anymore. I was praying, reading the scriptures, going to church, serving others, and doing the best I could, but to no avail. The feelings of being completely overwhelmed and unable to handle the smallest things in my day were getting me down.

A few weeks later, I went to my monthly doctor appointment to make sure all was still well with the pregnancy. As soon as my doctor walked in the door and asked me how I was doing, I emotionally fell apart. Loosing control of my emotions in front of someone besides my husband was totally unlike me! I just started to cry and began to express how I felt like I was going crazy. I was so embarrassed that I broke down in front of my doctor. Here is my journal entry relating this experience:

September 22, 2000

Okay, here it is: Lately I've been very down (if you haven't noticed from my previous entries). I worry about things that I never use to and little things are extremely overwhelming. I've been staying away from play group and other group activities. I have also been screening all my calls. The only people I've wanted to talk to are my husband and sometimes my mom. I just figured it was all the pregnancy. Then I started to notice that things I usually really enjoy are not fun to me anymore. This is when I began to realize my feelings were not normal.

I decided to talk to my doctor even though this was incredibly difficult for me. I hate looking weak! She made me take a little test in her office. It wasn't very fair because I couldn't cheat on the answers. There were several questions stating, "On a level from 1–10 how do you feel about yourself, your life, and do you enjoy things you use to," and on and on and on. I knew I needed to be honest, but man, was that a challenge! After I was done, she came in, reviewed my answers, totaled up the numbers, and proceeded to inform me that I am severely depressed.

My doctor wants me to see a counselor and possibly get on medication so it doesn't get worse. I'm really having a hard time accepting that I'm a basket case. I know I should look at it as an illness that has been stirred up by all the hormones, but I can't get past the feeling that only weak people need counseling and medications. I keep hoping it's all a bad dream and I'm going to wake up being my strong, happy self. Unfortunately, it hasn't happened yet.

I think maybe I should just reduce all the added stress in my life and focus only on me and my family. Sometimes I feel okay about giving up the service I am providing at church because in doing so, maybe I can avoid taking medication. But after today, I feel like I should be sent to a loony bin! I wish it was clearer to me what I should do. Actually, I really wish it would all go away or that I could get past my pride enough to see what I need to do.

This probably doesn't make much sense. Not making sense is normal nowadays. I just thought I would take advantage of the time I had and fill you in on what's been going on.

As you can see, my personal storm was forming, but I was not going to have anything to do with it. I was in complete denial.

Brainstorming Challenge: Have you noticed signs of your storm forming? What are they? Are you accepting them for what they are or pretending they are something else?

_____

_____

_____

_____

_____

CHAPTER 3

TRIGGERS

O NCE A STORM BEGINS TO FORM OVER THE OCEAN, CONVERGING winds trigger numerous thunderstorms. As stated earlier, these thunderstorms are the beginning sign of a potential hurricane. I find it interesting that it's the "converging" winds that trigger the thunderstorms. Another word for "converging" is to "close in." How often do you feel that way? Trapped and closed in? For me personally, when I feel closed in, it triggers me and my storm begins to gather strength just like the formation of a hurricane.

At this time in my life, I was nowhere near ready to accept the diagnosis of depression. In my mind, at this stage, depression was just another way of saying someone was weak, not full of faith, or not willing to fight for happiness. It was just an excuse for not getting out of bed in the morning and I was not going to have any part of it! I would fight these feelings and I would conquer! I didn't need help or medication. I was faithful; I was righteous, and no one, not even this stupid diagnosis, was going to prove otherwise.

Despite my best efforts, I couldn't hide from the inevitable. I was depressed and even though I wasn't going to admit it, I knew it showed in my face and countenance. No matter how hard I tried putting on a happy face, I knew I wasn't fooling many. I constantly told others that life was fantastic even though I felt like I was dying inside. I was so embarrassed and ashamed of my weakened state of mind. I began avoiding people even more because it took so much effort to pretend to be happy and satisfied with life. This ongoing act was exhausting!

October 1, 2000

The hardest Sunday I've had. During our church meeting, it took everything in me not to bolt out the door and go home. The only reason I didn't is because I was teaching a children's Sunday school class right after.

I didn't want to talk to anyone or have anyone talk to me. I didn't even want to pass them in the halls. In fact, before the meeting was over, I got up and went into the bathroom to hide. While there I had a major panic attack. When it was over, I came out of the bathroom and saw people still in the hallway, so I went outside and around the building to avoid them.

I think part of my deal is that people are learning that I'm having this problem. As a result, everyone that looked at me today or I passed in the hall, I thought to myself, "Do they know?" I felt so out of place and so exposed. I'm glad we won't be at church next week.

As you can see, one of my triggers was looking weak in others' eyes. I didn't want to be pitied or treated any differently because of a stupid diagnosis. I didn't want people to avoid me because they didn't know how to act around me and treated me like I might break. I was embarrassed and ashamed that I had allowed such weakness to take over and I feared people could see right through my fake smile. This caused sheer panic! Many times I experienced panic attacks. My breathing would become quick and short, like I was hyperventilating. My heart would pound so hard it felt like it was going to burst. These panic attacks were terrifying. To avoid these attacks and the feelings of inadequacy, embarrassment, shame, and worthlessness, I stopped answering the phone, hanging out with friends, and spent more time in bed than usual. I did whatever I could think of to remain as hidden as possible. Sometimes I recognized what I was doing as acts of avoiding and hiding. However, other times, I didn't understand or see clearly that what I was doing was not only hiding from others, but trying to hide from the unpleasant feelings that consumed me daily.

Brainstorming Challenge: What are your triggers? What are you hiding from? How are you hiding? Are you sleeping too much, avoiding friends and family, playing video games constantly, watching YouTube, or participating in social media all the time in order to numb your feelings? Make a list below of your triggers and how you are hiding:

_____

_____

_____

_____

_____

_____

_____

_____

CHAPTER 4

ORGANIZATION AND FORMATION OF A STORM

As TRIGGERS SET OFF THUNDERSTORMS, THE THUNDERSTORMS begin to organize and strengthen, bringing about the formation of a hurricane — the greatest storm on earth.

November 14, 2000

I didn't write last night because I wasn't in the mood and very tired. I was at my parents' house and had a huge anxiety attack. I felt as though everything was crashing down on me and I felt totally out of control. My dad walked in from work at this point and immediately sat down by my side. He hugged me, listened to me, and talked to me. It helped in more ways than I can describe. Today I feel a bit better. It just feels like that little light at the end of the tunnel is getting smaller and smaller. I just want it to end; to have it all in the past. It's so exhausting to constantly deal with it every hour of every day and still try to lead a normal life. I feel like I am clinging to a dirt wall. My body aches from holding on so tightly. I can see a small opening above, but I'm so tired that no matter how hard I try, I can't move closer to it. At the same time, I feel as if something is grabbing my ankles and trying to pull me down farther into this bottomless pit. All my energy and strength is being used just to stay in that one place. It's terrifying. I feel so helpless. It's dark and cold, and lonely. How do I inch upward to the light? How do I just endure?

For me, the organization and strengthening that formed my storm was the incredible amount of anger I felt toward God. I was furious with Him! Here I was doing what God had asked of me, having another baby even though I wasn't ready, and this was the thanks I got? I felt utterly betrayed by the one individual I thought I could trust the most. My heart was crushed and my anger increased daily.

Little did I know, being diagnosed with depression was just the beginning. Within a few months after the diagnosis, I went into preterm labor while visiting family in Utah. My husband and I had brought our family to visit for Thanksgiving and while visiting, decided to accept a job position in Utah in order to be close to our extended family again. The day we were to get on the airplane to return to Florida, I went into labor. As a result, I spent five days in the hospital and when released, lived with my in-laws in their home on strict bed rest for the remaining three months of my pregnancy. Meanwhile my husband went back to Florida with my parents, packed up our house, and moved us to Utah.

November 26, 2000 (written in hindsight)

We are about to go home to Florida to move back to Utah. I know it's the right thing to do, but I am so sad to be leaving my friends and my counselor. However, I will be brave. I have two weeks to see them and wrap up the past three and a half years we've lived there.

I begin to feel awful. I think it's a result of last night's dinner. This pregnancy has been hard and moving in the middle of it isn't going to make it any easier. I go outside to walk with my husband hoping it will make me feel better. Instead, I feel worse. Our plane leaves in three hours. We go to the Emergency Room just to be safe. They say I'm in labor. I'm rushed by ambulance to another hospital where I stay for five days. I then go back to my in-laws' house where I lay on the couch for another three months.

Again I say, "Why?" God could prevent this. Why didn't He? Is it so wrong to want to say goodbye and pack my own house? Why am I being punished? I feel low, discouraged, worthless, unloved, alone, afraid, and lots and lots of anger. I have lost trust. I have lost control. My faith in God and my relationship with Him before this preterm labor was not fantastic. I was frustrated with Him. But now, I am furious! I see Him as a mean, unkind, "sit up in heaven and laugh at me" kind of God. I don't trust Him anymore. I feel defeated.

December 6, 2000

Sorry I haven't been writing. It's not like there's a lot going on in my life right now and I don't want to write…laid on the couch all day again…everyday. This morning my mom leaves for Florida. I'm sad. I think it's more because I wish it was me that was going. I want to pack up my house. I want to say goodbye. I want to be up and around.

December 7, 2000

A rough morning. My mom called with a question about packing and everything seemed to hit me. I'm really going to miss my house and Florida. Tonight the baby's been kicking so hard. It hurts! My oldest child has been struggling a bit. She said she doesn't want a baby anymore. This was when I couldn't come eat with her at the table. We talked a little and I think she feels better. It's a constant struggle, but together, we will make it through a day at a time.

I can't begin to put into words the amount of anger and betrayal I felt in relationship to God. How could He be so mean? Wasn't I doing my best? Wasn't I doing His will over mine? Why did my family have to be a part of this punishment? I felt He was just looking down at me laughing at the pain and frustration I was experiencing. God quickly lost His status as my friend and became my enemy instead.

Brainstorming Challenge: What is forming your storm? Is it sadness, betrayal, anger, hopelessness, fear, doubt? Reach deep inside and pinpoint the emotions that are organizing and forming your storm.

_____

_____

_____

_____

_____

_____

_____

_____

_____

_____

_____

CHAPTER 5

CHAIN REACTIONS AND STAGES OF DEVELOPMENT

SOMETHING INTERESTING ABOUT THE FORMATION AND EVENTUAL development of hurricanes is that it begins with something quite small. However, due to a chain reaction of events, it increases in formation and strength. One thing leads to another, and certain conditions spark in response to something else and then that triggers another response. Before long, a 'feedback mechanism' has occurred and what was once a small storm disturbance has become a full-fledged hurricane.

Little did I know but I was in a feedback mechanism of my own. Have you ever noticed that when one thing goes wrong, everything else seems to follow? It's like dominos. I remember, as a child, painstakingly setting up a huge line of dominos and almost reaching the end of the process, when something would hit that first one and they would all come tumbling down. It was so infuriating!

My anger in regard to my situation was just like those dominos. It fueled my anger toward God and that anger led to feelings of worthlessness which then led to feelings of being unable to be loved. My self worth was disappearing at an incredible rate. It didn't matter how much people would tell me they loved me or thought I was awesome, I didn't believe them. I constantly accused my husband of just saying he loved me because he had to due to our marriage. It wasn't so much that I was being stubborn; I honestly couldn't understand how people could possibly see me as awesome or beautiful, or love me for that matter, when I was so dark inside.

May 27, 2001

Who is this person I'm becoming? I hate everything about her! She's angry, frustrated, and wants nothing to do with her family, who are her main support. I hate this woman. What's wrong with me? Why does every little thing bother me? If I acted on my impulses, I would trash this house and run away. It takes everything in me to hold myself back. When I look at pictures of my high school days, I see someone I don't know anymore. It's as if I'm looking at someone else's pictures.

I'm getting so tired of fighting this battle. It seems no matter how hard I try, I just get trampled on. What kind of a mother and wife am I? I'm neither. I'm just an empty shell, a zombie that goes about the day in a trance.

Who wants to live with something like that?

September 2, 2001

Why do I constantly feel I know what others are thinking about me? I seem to do this only with people who I really care for — my husband, my mom and dad, and especially my Heavenly Father. Why am I always second guessing Him? Why do I feel He is sensitive and understanding to everyone else but me? Why do I feel unworthy of His love and comfort? Is it because I don't want it? Am I still too angry? Am I afraid of being betrayed? Am I afraid of being asked to give so much again? How do I get out of this circle of destruction?

A poem I wrote March 14, 2001

LOST

The girl I once was is gone.
I'm lost, afraid, confused.
Where is she?
It seems so long ago I embraced her
And loved her
But somehow, somewhere
She disappeared
My heart aches.
I long to hear her laughter
To feel her joys
Carefree. Fun.
I wonder if she'll ever return?
I stumble around in darkness.
She must return!
I can't live without her
Scared, alone, lost
My head constantly spinning
Feeling nothing
Void.

Please help me find that little girl.
What if I continue to become ugly inside?
What kind of man could possibly live with that?
Who would expect him to?
My children never having a fun mom
Someone who will play with them
And be kind at times
How is that fair to them?
I want to be better…
But how?
I can't think clearly
I turn in circles
It's exhausting
Discouraging
Please help me find the real me…
Whoever she is.
And please, let me like her.

Brainstorm Challenge: What are the emotions or thoughts that are sparking your storm's chain reactions? Are you angry, frightened, lonely, or resentful? Do you feel worthless or unable to be loved? What do you think others are thinking about you? How do you feel about yourself personally? Do you see a pattern or common denominator?

_____

_____

_____

_____

_____

_____

PART 2

A Storm is Raging

CHAPTER 6

SUSTAINING STRENGTH

Once a hurricane has formed, it naturally provides a way to stay strong by forcing the pressure that's building at the top of the cyclone to flow outward from the center. A chimney type formation keeps the heavier pressure from piling up around the center by continuously diverting the air off to either side of it. If the pressure were to fall inside the center, the storm would ultimately weaken or could even be destroyed. As a result, nature finds a way to keep the storm going strong by preventing this collapse from happening.

Anger was my personal chimney that kept my storm strong. It sounds crazy now, but at the time, staying angry felt like the only way I could protect myself from collapsing. If I let my guard down, if I began to trust God again, I would just get crushed. Besides, I was in no mood to try and change at this point. I was too angry. I remember visiting a new counselor shortly after moving back to

Utah. After explaining my anger toward God and how I had felt abandoned by Him, this counselor told me to read the scriptures, pray, and serve others in order to feel better. What?! Did she not just hear what I said? I could barely get out of bed and serve my own children, let alone someone else, and there was no way I was ready to turn to God for help. I was furious! Thankfully, my counselor in Florida had taught me that it was okay to keep searching for a counselor I felt a connection with and that I didn't have to go to the first one I found. As I look back at the anger that kept my storm strong, I realize I misunderstood what was really happening. I falsely believed that by holding onto anger I was freeing myself from guilt and staying safe from hurt and disappointment, when in reality, I was just imprisoning myself, locking the door and throwing away the key.

September 2, 2001

I feel like all my life I've been forced to do what is right. Not by my parents or leaders, but by me! If I don't want to go to church or read the scriptures or pray, then I feel that I am a disappointment to God. How do I stop this kind of thinking?

I feel like I'm stuck on a rollercoaster and it's too much stress and confusion! It's going too fast! But I can't get off. It makes me angry, frustrated, and scared. I don't know how to slow it down so I can enjoy the ride. Although I think I want to get off this ride, I know that's not entirely true. The gospel of Jesus Christ is what I want in my life, but it's too hard right now. I'm so confused. I feel entirely lost and completely disoriented.

Unfortunately, anger toward God was not the only anger I felt. I was, of course, angry at myself for not being able to pull myself out of this nightmare I was living, but I also turned my anger on my sweet husband.

April 15, 2001

I am so angry with my husband and my heart is broken at the same time. I'm SO tired and my throat is tight. Today has been one of the worst days as far as depression goes. I actually had an anxiety attack on the freeway while my husband was driving and, of course, no one noticed. We got home and my husband went straight to bed. Why is he so blind to the obvious? So many times lately I feel that he just doesn't care. Maybe he's burned out. He says he loves me and he hugs and kisses me, but that's not what I need. I don't want affection or pity. I want support and help without asking for it all the time. Asking just makes me feel weaker and like more of a failure.

Oh, I am so tired of living in this hell. I feel so much anger and unhappiness that my gut is turning inside out constantly. I want to run away, but where do I go? Besides, how can I leave my children? They need me.

I didn't recognize it at the time, but what I was really doing was finding any way I could to keep the storm I was experiencing going strong. Why? I feel it was because my storm had become familiar. It wasn't comfortable living in my storm, it wasn't fun, but it was all I knew, and the thought of stepping into the unknown scared me even more than experiencing the nightmare I was living inside the chaos. Another reason I chose to hold on to anger was because deep down I felt I deserved this unhappiness. I was angry with God. Who is angry with God that's a good person? I was so convinced that I was wicked, and wicked people did not deserve happiness and peace.

July 8, 2001

I'm outside on the church lawn. I'm amazed I'm even here. I didn't want to come to church at all, but felt like it's where the Lord wanted me today. I don't know why. All church does is upset me even more.

A car just drove by while I was walking from my car to this spot on the grass. Someone in the car yelled, "Satan loves you." My first response, "Yeah, I know." It's so much easier to believe that than it is to believe God loves me. I feel worthy of Satan's love (if there is such a thing).

In church today, they were discussing how it takes time to become like Christ and that our trials make us stronger and help put us on a path toward God, but does it take ages for this to happen? How can anyone do it? Yet, when I say that, I feel like such a whiner. But truthfully, I'm so afraid. At times I feel like I have no choice. I can't get off this ride. It's either hell or exhaustion. Is it worth it? I can't feel anymore. I can't keep up encouragement and desire.

Brainstorming Challenge: What are you doing to keep your storm strong? Are you holding on to an emotion or past situation? You may not recognize what you are doing right away, but I challenge you to dig deep. Pray and ask God to help you understand how you are preventing the collapse of your personal storm. It's not easy to recognize or admit what is keeping your storm strong, but once you acknowledge it, it actually strengthens you so much more than the false strength you are holding on to.

CHAPTER 7

THE INTENSITY SCALE

Master, with anguish of spirit
I bow in my grief today.
The depths of my sad heart are troubled.
Oh, waken and save, I pray!
Torrents of sin and of anguish
Sweep o'er my sinking soul,
And I perish! I perish! dear Master.
Oh, hasten and take control!

(*Hymns*. "Master, the Tempest Is Raging," 105, vs. 2.
Words by Mary Ann Baker, music by H.R. Palmer)

EVERY HURRICANE HAS A CATEGORY THAT INDICATES THE INTENsity or strength of that particular storm. While we were living in Florida, we actually had several hurricanes that we encountered. Most of them were a category 1, which means that the wind speed reaches 74–95 miles per hour. Evacuation is not necessary for a storm this size, but there is still quite a bit of damage that can occur.

With each rise in category, the wind speeds increase. A category 2 hurricane has wind speeds between 96–100 miles per hour; category 3 is 111–130 miles per hour; category 4 is 131–155 miles per hour; and finally, a category 5 has wind speeds reaching over 155 miles per hour.

Something I didn't realize until I lived in Florida, was that not only do you have to fear the hurricane itself, but the hundreds of tornadoes that accompany the outskirts of the storm. When we first moved to Florida, it was hurricane season. I had grown up in Utah where the only thing to really fear was the dreaded earthquake that was bound to happen any day. Our oldest child was just barely a year old when we arrived in our new home. The floor plan of the home we lived in had the master bedroom on one side of the house and all the other bedrooms on the opposite side of the house. One night after putting our one year old in bed, I went to bed but couldn't sleep. For some unknown reason, I felt very unsettled and frightened. This was several years before the depression diagnosis and it was very unlike me to worry about nothing. I kept telling myself to chill out and calm down, there was no danger. Finally, to put my mind at ease, I prayed and asked God to surround our home with His angels. I felt peace come over me and I was finally able to sleep.

The next morning, as I was feeding our oldest breakfast, I turned on the news. Immediately I understood my uneasy feelings from the night before. Every county surrounding ours was hit by multiple tornadoes throughout the night.

In Florida, there are no basements. I had always figured that if you lived where tornadoes were an issue, you could run to the root cellar like they did on *The Wizard of Oz*. There are no root cellars in Florida due to being at sea level. As I watched the news, I cried as I heard of a grandmother who was holding on to the bottom of the toilet with one arm and grasping her grandchild with the other. She held as tight as she could, but the wind was so strong that the child was ripped from her arms. Thankfully and miraculously, her grandchild was found in a tree several miles away safe and sound. Realizing the danger and fierceness of these storms brought a fear beyond anything I had experienced before. How does one stay safe when there's nowhere to go that is safe?

This type of terror is exactly how I felt as my personal storm became not only a hurricane, but a category 5 hurricane.

One day in Sunday school, we were discussing Noah and his ark. I immediately had a scene from the Disney movie, *Fantasia 2000*, come to mind where Donald Duck is portraying Noah. Noah and his family are finally closing everything up and the rain has become a furious flood. Suddenly, a woodpecker begins pecking into the side of the ark. With each hole the woodpecker makes, water begins to pour into the ark. Donald (Noah) is frantically trying to cover the holes with his hands and feet, but with every hole he covers, the woodpecker makes a new one and the water continues to pour in.

This was the perfect analogy of my life at that time. I was trying to stay above water. I felt I was holding on by the tips of my fingernails, yet something would always come along and try to sink me, just like that woodpecker. I was beyond tired. I noticed a change in myself. I was starting to give up. Every day became darker. Every day became harder. Every day I longed for it all to STOP!

May 17, 2001 (8:52 AM)

Why do I wake up this way? Today I don't want to exist. It would be so much easier to just stay asleep. I forced myself to get in the shower and open the blinds in my window. That felt like too much. How am I supposed to function? How am I supposed to take care of my family? Such simple tasks overwhelm me. I wish I could just sleep....that I could be alone. How am I going to get through this day?

May 20, 2001

Regarding the last entry...I didn't get through that day without a lot of help. And even with that help, I barely survived.

I'm glad I took time to write what I did Thursday. My feelings of exhaustion and being overwhelmed increased. So much so, that just moving the smallest amount physically hurt so much. I kept thinking how nice it would be to take a bunch of pills, lie down, and sleep. The scariest thing about those thoughts was that the voice that is usually in the background telling me that it wouldn't solve anything was gone.

I felt a strong impression to move downstairs, to get out of my room where the pills were so easily accessible. I knew if I went down the stairs, I wouldn't come back up because my body hurt so much. As hard as it was, I did this and once I was downstairs, I called my husband and told him to get home right away! I knew I couldn't be alone. I didn't trust myself at all.

While my husband was home, he contacted a counselor that my family had suggested. He wanted to talk to me on the phone and

I did not want that at all! He wouldn't hang up until he heard my voice so I finally agreed. Never have I cried to my counselors, but I couldn't help it. I was at the lowest I'd ever been. He wanted to see me that night, so at 6:00 pm, I met with him. For an hour and a half, I cried and told him everything I could think of. He was so easy to talk to and really cared and understood. Although it was very difficult, I feel it was a good thing I went to the counselor right away because I didn't hold anything in.

I pray that those of you reading this book have never experienced this before, but if you have or if you are currently, please seek help from someone! This is so incredibly important that I plead with you to take the following challenge!

Challenge: If you feel like there is no hope and that life is not worth living, or if you feel the world would be better off without you, tell someone right now! Put this book down and tell someone! Call a friend, family member, church leader, or call this number: 1-800-273-TALK (8255) for the National Suicide Hotline that operates 24/7.

Even if you are not currently feeling this way, but have recently, tell someone! I know it's hard. I know it's embarrassing. I know it sucks to have to seek help when you don't necessarily think you need it, want it, or deserve it, but trust me... *tell someone immediately!*

Important: If you have a friend reach out to you about suicidal thoughts, this is one secret to **never** keep! Tell a trusted adult *immediately*!

Brainstorm Challenge: Think of people you trust that you can talk to. Also make a list of ways to keep your environment safe. For example, who could you ask to remove any items that could be a threat to your safety? You could also make a list of places you could go until you feel safe again. Have a plan in place and list it here:

_____

_____

_____

_____

_____

_____

_____

_____

_____

_____

_____

_____

_____

_____

_____

_____

_____

_____

_____

_____

You need to let someone know and have a prevention plan in place. Even if you are not planning on acting on it, let someone know you have been thinking about it. Don't read on, unless you do this. Seriously!

CHAPTER 8

Storm Surges

ALTHOUGH THE DAY I SERIOUSLY CONSIDERED TAKING MY LIFE was an incredibly dark day, it also became a turning point. Not right away, but over time. I began meeting with a counselor again and started taking medication. I wasn't thrilled with the idea of medication, but I needed help. My life literally depended on it, and as you will see, so did my family's lives.

Did you know that the most destructive part of a hurricane is not actually the storm itself? The most destructive part is what accompanies it—storm surges. As a hurricane moves closer to land, heavy rain, strong winds, and tornadoes begin, and although these are dangerous, the most catastrophic are the storm surges. A storm surge is a dome of ocean water that can be 50 to 100 miles wide. As it hits land, it demolishes piers, boardwalks, marinas, homes, and other structures along the coast. It also erodes beaches, streets, and railroads.

Why am I including this part of the hurricane process? Up until this point in my life of depression, I had focused on *me* and the way my storm was affecting *my* life. Little did I know how much danger my family was in as potential storm surges from my storm were threatening their well-being.

When I was suicidal, I felt that taking my life would be a gift I could give my family. I felt I was such a huge burden and they deserved so much more. My husband didn't sign up for a depressed and useless wife. My children didn't deserve to grow up with a mom that could barely get out of bed in the morning. What better gift than to give them their freedom from me?

I look back at those thoughts and am chilled to the bone. I was so confused. I was so deceived. Let me share with you what opened my eyes.

April 26, 2002

I have to give you an update. Sorry, but it's going to be quick because I have to get the kids ready for school.

Tuesday I was having a terrible day! I haven't been doing very well for the past week or two, but Tuesday, it all came to a head. I called my mom and cried for two hours to her. I was telling her how I didn't understand why I feel so dissatisfied with my life. I have everything I've wanted and more. Why did I feel trapped? Why did I resent my children and husband? I went on and on and on. We talked about several things, but none of them seemed to help. Suddenly my mom said something to this effect, "Kimberly, I know you don't want to hear this, but I am telling you, everything you are feeling is what Satan wants you to feel." I thought to myself, "Yeah, yeah, I know. You've said this before, but how is it going to help or make any difference?" Then my mom said this, "Satan doesn't want you to succeed because he knows your children are valiant spirits. He also doesn't want your marriage to succeed." At that moment, a light came on and I realized that Satan was getting to my family through me! To tell you the blunt and honest truth, I was ticked off! No one messes with my family!!!

I am so grateful for my mom and her courage in coming forward. In the past, whenever she mentioned the "Satan was doing it" kind of stuff, I bit her head off. I am grateful for God helping me to be more receptive. It terrifies me to think how these thoughts I've allowed Satan to put in my head could have affected my family forever.

Now do you see why I have included storm surges? When you are in the center of your own nightmarish storm, you don't realize or recognize the potential damage hovering over your loved ones, be it family, friends, etc. I understood that depression was an illness that affects how one thinks and feels, so I wasn't about to blame depression on Satan. What occurred to me for the first time that particular day, was that Satan may not cause depression, but he does use it to his advantage. I wish I could adequately put into words how grateful I am that I am still here. I look at my family now and, despite the many years of my storm, I am a better person because of them and I know they are better because of me. I may not have been the best mom in the world, but I understand what a bad day feels like and I understand how sometimes you just need a hug and *not* advice. I am so thankful that I did not let Satan win by listening to and believing all the lies he was feeding me. I didn't know it at the time and I still don't see the whole picture, but I know I am here for a reason and so does Satan. He is persistent, but I am more determined than he is!

Brainstorming Challenge: Why does Satan want you out of the picture? What lasting effects would result if you were not around? How would it affect your loved ones? How could it affect your future family?

_____

_____

_____

_____

_____

_____

_____

_____

_____

_____

_____

_____

_____

_____

_____

_____

_____

_____

_____

_____

_____

_____

_____

_____

_____

_____

_____

CHAPTER 9

THE EYE OF THE STORM

O NE OF THE CRAZIEST PHENOMENA OF A HURRICANE IS THE EYE of the storm. Surrounding the eye is utter chaos and destruction, but inside the eye is the calmest part of the storm. I remember experiencing this strange phenomenon during one of the hurricanes that hit Florida while we were living there. The wind and rain were immense! The power was out, the thunder was deafening, and lightning was striking all around, then everything suddenly calmed down. It was kind of eerie. If it wasn't for the fact that we knew we were in the middle of the eye, I would have thought the storm was over. Within a few minutes, however, the quiet ended and the chaos returned.

I compare this part of a hurricane to the time in my own storm where I decided to just accept that I had depression and was most likely going to live with it for the rest of my life. It wasn't that I had given up; it was that I decided I needed to accept it in order to fight for my family. I began reading every self-help book I could. I continued to pray (something I never stopped doing, even when I was furious with God), and I continued going to church. There were times where I felt I was getting a grasp on life again, but these times of relief always seemed to be short-lived.

April 13, 2002

Today I felt God's love for me while at church. This is the second big milestone in a week. How come? Not that I'm complaining, but have I done anything different? I know everything I've gone through, good and bad, has helped me get here, but I really feel the number one thing that has helped me, as far as religion is concerned, is that somehow I have humbled myself and allowed myself to be teachable. Does that make any sense?

I don't deny that I have hardened my heart. I was so angry and hurt that I didn't want to be kind or teachable out of rebellion. I didn't want to open myself up to be hurt again. Life is so hard, and though it sounds crazy, I felt that if I could close up my heart, life would be easier. There would be no chance of feeling hurt, betrayed, guilty, or unworthy of love. This past Sunday, for the first time in two years, I felt inner peace — the calming, restful, happiness.

I am so afraid it's going to disappear, these feelings of desire. Feeling the desire to learn, serve, love, and trust. I'm going to do everything I can to keep this little flame growing, but my little flames are so easily extinguished. Please, please stay!

This constant ache for happiness and the uncertainty that came when happiness appeared pretty much describes where I existed for the next fifteen years. It was one battle after another. I would be stable on a certain medication until my body would adapt and I would have to try a new medication. Some medications worked right away and others made things so much worse, but I continued to push on. I also had times where counseling was necessary and other times where it wasn't needed. I experienced times of peace and happiness, but it was a huge battle to get there and it never lasted very long. I moved through life with a fake smile on my face and a vow that I would never give up for my family's sake. I fought for my family. I felt like I was on a continuous rollercoaster ride of ups and downs.

Here are a few journal entries to show you what it was like to be in the eye of my storm.

February 8, 2003

Quick entry: I am dreading church tomorrow for no particular reason. This happens every week. I really think it would just be easier to go inactive, but I can't. The scary thing is that I see that I really can, but I'm trying to be strong and very careful not to let this desire win.

December 23, 2001

You know, today, I'm actually looking forward to going to church. On top of that, I am starting to get excited about Christmas. Maybe it's because of the feelings I've had the past few days. About two weeks ago I started going downhill. I started feeling the same old things – not wanting to get out of bed, not wanting to face the day, cranky, sad, and unhappy.

Last week my husband and I discussed my feelings of anger and fear and lack of trust toward God. He said the same thing I'd been feeling for some time; I need to humble myself... but how? How do I humble myself and just start trusting the Lord when I'm afraid of what He might do?

As I read the scriptures this past week, I came across a quote I'd written that says that with faith, the power of the universe can help you in your hour of need and in solutions to problems too great for your human strength and intelligence.

I need help solving this depression problem, but I lack faith. It didn't seem fair. Then, Wednesday night I saw the tail end of a TV show and one of the characters told this story to a friend having some emotional difficulties:

One day a man was walking and fell into a man hole. A doctor walked by and the man yelled to him for help. The doctor wrote him a prescription and threw it down to him. A while later, a priest walks by and again, the man calls for help. The priest writes him a prayer and throws it down to him. Then his best friend walks by and the man yells up to him for help. The friend jumps into the man hole. The man looks at his friend and says, "Are you stupid? Now we are both stuck down here!" His friend looks at him and says, "Yes, but I've been here before and know the way out."

This story touched me and I heard a soft voice telling me Jesus is that friend and He will get you through this even if He has to carry you himself. These feelings were very subtle, but they were there! I feel my heart softening a little. I pray it will continue so I can trust and love and not be ashamed of feeling so angry. I'm very grateful for this experience and I promise I will not give up! I will find my faith again!

December 12, 2014

I've been on the verge of tears all day. I'm heartbroken and angry, but I don't want to go into detail. Going to lunch with my friend was the best part of my day. I'm scared because every time I take medication for my headaches, I contemplate taking a ton to just try to feel better and escape/run away from certain people and situations. My little family is my rock and I owe my determination to keep fighting to them. I love them so much!

March 24, 2015

I am completely over stimulated and agitated. I'm ornery, overwhelmed, and tired. I want to cry, scream, throw a tantrum, and stomp my feet. Unfortunately, that last one is still not possible because I'm still wearing my foot brace. My foot hurts, my body is tired, and I am drained! How is it that a combination of small, unexpected things can cause me to feel totally out of control? Granted, I felt overwhelmed this morning about all I had to do today, but the small, unexpected stuff just about put me over the edge. I hate being like this! I hate being weak and fragile! It is not my nature!!!

During the eye of my storm, things were not as chaotic as before, but they weren't sunshiny and bright. There were ups and downs, times of stillness and times of showers. I figured this was going to be my life forever. Although it wasn't ideal, I was willing to stick it out for the sake of my family. Because of them, I kept going and because of them, my eyes were finally opened to the truth about the storm I was living. Because I didn't quit, God led me to exactly who I needed to help me discover what I was missing out on. I knew I was missing out, that's why I was not thrilled with the thought of living in this stage of my storm for the rest of my life, but I had no idea what I was looking for or, more importantly, how to get it.

Brainstorming Challenge: Who are you fighting for? Do you feel a sense of missing out on something better? Do you feel happiness is within your grasp, but don't know how to grab it? Do you believe you are of worth? Do you want to not only believe it, but **know** it? Write your thoughts here:

PART 3

BREAKING FREE

CHAPTER 10

THE EYE WALL

An interesting fact about hurricanes: surrounding the eye, the calmest part of the storm, is something scientists call the "eye wall." The eye wall is the most destructive part of the hurricane itself and is located on the side of the eye where the wind blows in the same direction as the storm is moving. Isn't that interesting? As the hurricane is moving forward, the winds on the side of its progressing movement are the strongest. I could relate. The harder I tried to move forward in life, the stronger the winds became. I felt defeated and despair started to consume me.

I had such a huge longing for peace and happiness. I figured it was not ever going to be a reality, but it didn't stop me from desiring it, hungering for it. I worked on building my relationship with God and I started seeing a counselor again in January 2015. It seemed the harder I tried to draw nearer to Christ, the harder my life became. Within a matter of a few months, my husband was asked to take on a huge service opportunity for our church, our daughter accepted an opportunity to travel and live far away for almost two years providing service to those in the area she was living, and my health took a turn for the worse. I eventually had gallbladder surgery, which kept me from attending our son's first season of parades with the high school band, and to make a sad story even sadder, our dog became sick and died. Yep, all hell was breaking loose. It was definitely a time of testing. Was I really committed to trusting God? Was I really ready to mend the relationship with Him and move forward?

At one of my counseling appointments, I was describing to my counselor how I felt stuck. I explained how it didn't seem to matter what I did, nothing was helping me move forward. I had the desire, I had the motivation, I didn't want to live this way anymore, but I couldn't stop feeling down. I happened to also mention that no matter how hard I tried to feel the Holy Ghost and God's love for me, all I could hear and feel was darkness and yelling, chaos, and noise. I felt like I was losing my mind.

My counselor, being the very wise man he is, and a man of God, saw the truth behind my statement. He followed God's prompting and began opening my eyes to what was really happening. As we talked, I began to understand that I was not just battling depression, but I was battling the adversary as well. For the first time since my mom told me about Satan trying to get to my family, I realized the truth and reality of this statement in regard to me. Satan didn't want *me* to be happy. He didn't want *me* to repair my relationship with God. I had been fighting for my family, but I needed to be fighting for *me* as well. It was at this point that I determined to understand my enemy's tactics and ways so as to be empowered and no longer made to be a fool who so easily fell into his traps.

Just like in every battle, it is advantageous to know the enemy's ways. If you understand the enemy's line of attack, tricks, strategies, and desires, you can prepare and avoid imprisonment and tragedy. Also, just like in every battle, you need to know and trust your commander. You need to understand He loves you, cares about your welfare and safety, and that you can put your life in His hands. As I began my study of the adversary, I was also studying intensely my commander, Jesus Christ. It has been over a year of study, but what I have learned has set me free. I am no longer a victim of a chaotic storm. Not only that, but I foresee the signs of storms headed my way, and through Christ's help, can sometimes divert them altogether! I'm not saying life is perfect, that it doesn't have its ups and downs—it does. But I have discovered how to escape life's storms quicker! Are you ready to be set free?

Brainstorming Challenge: If your storm could end today, how would you feel? Are you ready to be empowered so you can break free of your storm?

_____

_____

_____

_____

_____

_____

_____

_____

_____

_____

_____

CHAPTER 11

A SUBTLE DISTURBANCE

M Y ENTIRE LIFE I BELIEVED IN THE BATTLE OF GOOD AND EVIL. I
believed in God and that everything good came
from Him. I knew there was a devil because the scriptures
testified of it, but I figured he was always in the background and only really came forward when we made bad
choices. What I have come to understand is that I was not
giving Satan enough credit. He wants us to believe he's
just hanging out in the background when in reality, he is
right in our faces all the time! Life is full of disappointments, discouragements, and illnesses—such as depression—that is part of our mortal journey. However, Satan
and his army don't back off and give us a break when
things get tough. In fact, just the opposite happens. He
sees a weakness, a tough thing we are going through,
and kicks us hard and relentlessly while we are down. I
couldn't comprehend how someone could be so hateful
and vicious, and therefore resisted believing he was trying

to thwart my attempts at being happy. I knew I needed to know, for myself, if he really was this kind of being. I went to the scriptures and my eyes were opened in regard to his character. I realized that I had been imprisoned and bound without even realizing it. Let me share a few words and phrases that describe Satan's characteristics found in the scriptures:

- The great liar/deceiver
- Speaks with much flattery
- Steals away the hearts of men causing much confusion and dissension
- Seeks power over all
- Binds and imprisons; chains of hell
- Enemy of God
- Worker of darkness
- Stirs up the hearts of men; anger and hatred
- Everlasting destruction
- Leads away the souls of men
- Carries away captive to eternal misery and woe
- Seeks the misery of all
- Destroyer of peace

In regard to Satan's characteristics and nature, C.S. Lewis has said, "Like a good chess player, Satan is always trying to maneuver you into a position where you can save your castle only by losing your bishop" (C.S. Lewis, *The Weight of Glory*).

When I realized how Satan had tricked me, I was ticked! As I studied more of his characteristics, tactics, and plans, I began to see more and more how he had snuck in and the reason I had felt such a heavy darkness constantly around me. Let me explain something here; I know depression is real. I have lived it and continue to battle it. However, it is my opinion that the illness of depression causes feelings of sadness and despair whereas Satan and his army encourage the feelings of worthlessness, being unlovable, anger, and darkness. Why does this matter? It is fantastic news! By understanding what is real and what is not, we can be set free from the traps we have fallen into unknowingly! I still suffer with depression, but I have control over my worth, hope, and the light I feel. You can have this too! The first thing we need to do is become aware of how the enemy entraps us in the first place.

Satan is extremely sneaky. I remember as a youth reading an analogy about Satan's ability to sneak up on us or hide where we would least expect to find him. The analogy was written by a leader in The Church of Jesus Christ of Latter-day Saints, Boyd K. Packer, who visited South Africa and was about what he learned while on a safari there. I have always had a strong fascination with Africa and the animals that live there, so this analogy was perfect for me.

Mr. Packer explained that as the safari guide took him near a watering hole, he noticed the water was literally mud. As an elephant stepped in to drink, other animals would drink the water that seeped up though its foot prints. He observed the antelope darting anxiously toward and away from the watering hole and asked the guide why they were so nervous; there didn't seem to be any evidence of danger. The guide informed Mr. Packer that there were crocodiles in the watering hole, but he didn't believe him. How could a gigantic African crocodile be in there?

To prove his point, the guide drove the jeep around to the other side of the watering hole. Boyd K. Packer explains what happened next, "I couldn't see anything except the mud, a little water, and the nervous animals in the distance. Then all at once I saw it! — a large crocodile, settled in the mud, waiting for some unsuspecting animal to get thirsty enough to come for a drink. Suddenly I became a believer! When he (the guide) could see I was willing to listen, he continued with the lesson. 'There are crocodiles all over the park,' he said, 'not just in the rivers. We don't have any water without a crocodile somewhere near it, and you'd better count on it.'"

Mr. Packer goes on to say, "Those ahead of you in life have probed about the water holes a bit and raise a voice of warning about crocodiles. Not just the big, gray lizards that can bite you to pieces, but *spiritual crocodiles,* infinitely more dangerous, and more deceptive and less visible, even, than those well-camouflaged reptiles of Africa. These spiritual crocodiles can kill or mutilate your souls. They can destroy your peace of mind and the peace of mind of those who love you. Those are the ones to be warned against, and there is hardly a watering place in all of mortality now that is not infested with them." ("Spiritual Crocodiles," *Ensign*, May 1976, 30–31.)

Some of my "spiritual crocodiles" at this time included my quickness in blaming everything on God, others, and depression itself. I fell into the trap of believing I was lost and could never be found and it was through no fault of my own. I had a false belief of being a victim of my circumstances and didn't feel I needed help from anyone, especially God. As I explained earlier, I used anger as a means of protection. The problem was that life continued to happen and I would get thrown a curve ball which would cause my personal world to come crashing down and I would begin again to feel there was no use in trying because I would forever be a failure. I had been caught in Satan's trap and didn't even know it.

Brainstorming Challenge: How is Satan camouflaging himself in your life? How do your thoughts cycle? Are there certain things, situations, or people that trigger you? Ask God to help you as you begin opening your eyes to the truth.

_____

_____

_____

_____

_____

_____

_____

_____

_____

_____

_____

_____

_____

_____

_____

_____

_____

_____

CHAPTER 12

CHAINS OF HELL

February 26, 2015

I WANT TO WRITE ABOUT MY WEEKEND. *I KNOW WORDS WILL NOT DO* *it justice and I am not feeling great right now…I think I caught a cold from being at the school subbing Monday and Tuesday. So, bear with me please.*

Saturday was a bad day emotionally, and by bedtime, I felt like a piece of crap in the middle of the road and as valuable. I cried while my husband slept. I couldn't stop thinking of how worthless I was. I was upset with myself for being selfish, judgmental, prideful, rude, unkind, and I was sad that I may be holding my husband back spiritually. It was so bad; I couldn't stop the thoughts and therefore couldn't sleep. I wanted it all to end, but I knew that ending it wasn't an option. It would hurt my family too much. As I lay there, crying, tired, and feeling worthless, I prayed that God would help me. Suddenly, I visually saw in my mind these words, "You have much to give." Immediately I realized that Satan is working hard to break through my armor while I am struggling with depression.

I tried quoting a scripture that has helped me in the past while going to school, Philippians 4:13, "I can do all things through Christ which strengtheneth me," but it wasn't working. My abusive thoughts kept coming. Finally I remembered something my dad taught me one day while I was crying on his shoulder in the beginning years of this depression journey. He looked at me, reminded me of my Scottish stubbornness, and told me to hold my CIS shield high. When I asked him what CIS meant, he replied…CRAM IT SATAN! This became my mantra and I even had it engraved on a ring I wear daily. So, that night, I began repeating, "Cram it Satan," over and over and over again until I fell asleep.

The next night (Sunday), I was reminded at church that we need to pour out our hearts to God. So, Monday morning I did just that. I thanked the Lord for helping me to see that the battle I am facing is not just my depression and I prayed that angels might encircle me, to protect me from Satan's blows while I begin to heal myself and try to make my armor stronger. Long story short, I felt much better and on Wednesday, while I was at my counseling appointment, we discussed ways for me to work on remedies for my guilty and abusive self-talk. It's going to be difficult and will most likely take a long time, but I am willing to do what I need to. One other thing my counselor suggested was engraving something on the other side of my CIS ring since 'Cram it Satan' has a negative connotation. On my way home from the appointment, I contemplated what I needed to be reminded of constantly that was positive. I am happy to report that on that evening I dropped my ring off to a friend to engrave the letters, GLM on the other side of my ring. It stands for, 'GOD LOVES ME!'

In 2 Timothy 2:26 of the English Standard Version (ESV) Bible, we are encouraged to, "come to [our] senses and escape from the snare of the devil, after being captured by him to do his will." One of the most eye-opening experiences I had in relation to my new understanding of the adversary's tricks happened at a conference I attended in February 2016. The presenter, Kirk Duncan, President of 3 Key Elements, was discussing some of the ways Satan's chains can attach to us. As I was listening, I was thinking about how I felt chained down, but I couldn't understand why. I mean, yeah I was not the best person in regard to trusting God and relying on Him, but I was doing everything I could to fix that. I was a good person inside and I knew it. I had just been lost and was trying to find my way home. As my thoughts returned to the presentation, suddenly something Mr. Duncan said hit me like a bolt of lightning! He was comparing the chains that hold us down to the negative things we think and say about ourselves. With each negative thought, with each negative word, we were allowing another chain to be placed around us. I tried to focus on the rest of the presentation, but my mind was going a hundred miles per hour as I realized the truth of what was just said in relation to my own life.

It all goes back to the beginning of the storm. Remember the chain reactions? Scientists call them "feedback mechanisms." Our thoughts are our greatest feedback mechanism! If I am constantly telling myself that I am a looser, a failure, hopeless, useless, unloved, weak, the scum of the earth, and a total loss, it is going to tie me down and I am literally allowing the chains of hell to encircle and imprison me!

I never understood how these thoughts were harming me and preventing me from moving forward. In my mind, I felt that all these negative thoughts were true, so they were easy to believe. I mean, didn't my outside life and the fact that I couldn't function well prove the truthfulness of these feelings and thoughts?

Here's where Satan's slyness comes into play. As C.S. Lewis helps us understand in his book, *The Last Battle*, the devil mixes a little truth with a big lie in order to make it far stronger and much more believable. Think about it, if Satan was whispering something to you that was completely false, you wouldn't believe it as quickly or easily, but if he adds a little truth to the lie, it is immediately accepted because of that small percentage of truth. Let me give you some examples. One of the negative thoughts that constantly ran though my mind was that I was an awful mom. Most of that was a lie. I fed my kids, played with them, helped them with their homework, went to their different activities, and much more. However, because I had bad days where I didn't do all of those things very well, I believed the lie. Another lie that is still constantly being thrown my way is that I can't do this—write a book, teach others how to escape their storms, give others hope through helping them find Christ again. Satan knows I fear failure and disappointing others, but if I gave in to these lies, you would not be holding this book in your hands right now.

Do you remember what happens to a storm after the chain reaction or feedback mechanisms occur? The storm becomes more organized, develops into its various stages, begins to protect itself from destruction or weaknesses, increases in intensity, and becomes the greatest storm on earth!

Do you see the significance? Depression, trial, difficulties in life are all storms. They are like tropical depressions, but when we add negative thoughts and words about ourselves, we are adding fuel to the fire, and before we know it, our tropical depression has become a destructive, horrifying hurricane! So, how do we stop it? That's what I want to share with you now. This particular exercise is what started my escape from my storm and continues to help me every day. Please, please do it!

Challenge: The Evidence Notebook

I am a huge fan of detective books, movies, and TV shows. One character in particular I love is Sherlock Holmes. Just like any good detective, we are going to gather evidence of Satan's attempts to stop us from progressing, experiencing peace, worth, love, and happiness. Here's how it works:

1. Get a notebook that you are able to carry with you at all times. I personally use one that is small and easily fits in my pocket or bag.

2. Title it: My Evidence Notebook

3. Every time you have a negative thought come to your mind, get out your notebook, put the date at the top of the page, number the entry, and record your thought word for word. Each time a new negative thought manifests, continue with the next number and write it down.

Here's an example:

Date:
#1: negative thought
#2: negative thought

#3: negative thought

The next day, continue where you left off, but be sure to include the new date:

Date:
#4: negative thought
#5: negative thought

Don't be surprised if you get a lot in one day. I remember when I started I usually had an average of 15–20 thoughts per day.

Note: Don't let anyone read it! EVER! If someone reads what you have written, those negative thoughts will become theirs. Please, don't spread the chains.

The more you collect this evidence, the more empowered you become. You will begin to distinguish lies quicker, and as a result, dismiss them immediately. Be warned however, Satan is not one to give up easily. A favorite quote of mine is by C.S. Lewis, "The enemy will not see you vanish into God's company without an effort to reclaim you." (C.S. Lewis, *Yours, Jack*)

Why do I bring this up? You will find that as you get better at stopping negative thoughts about yourself from entering your mind, someone else will try to put them there.

Let me give you an example. After I had been working on gathering my own evidence and recording it in my evidence notebook for several months, my son was frustrated with me and said something I had written in my notebook previously—almost word for word. He had no idea the words he used were words Satan had been trying to get me to believe. Instead of being upset with what he said, I shouted for joy! It freaked him out a little because he was expecting my feelings to be hurt. Instead, I saw it as a huge accomplishment! Satan knew he wasn't getting through my thoughts anymore, so he was trying to use others' words to convince me. I grabbed my notebook, wrote the date, the negative expression, and my son's name next to it with a big smiley face! This was a victory in my eyes and I actually thanked my son for his help. I was grateful for the experience and held no hard feelings toward him at all; however, I did remind him that respect is expected in our home, so not to plan on the same happy reaction if it happened again.

Are you going to take the challenge? A written commitment is more powerful than just thinking it or even speaking it, so below I want you to write your commitment. Are you going to get your own Evidence Notebook? When? Are you going to use it every day and every time you have a negative thought about yourself? After you have written this commitment, sign and date it, then go get your notebook and start collecting evidence!

_____

_____

_____

_____

_____

_____

_____

_____

_____

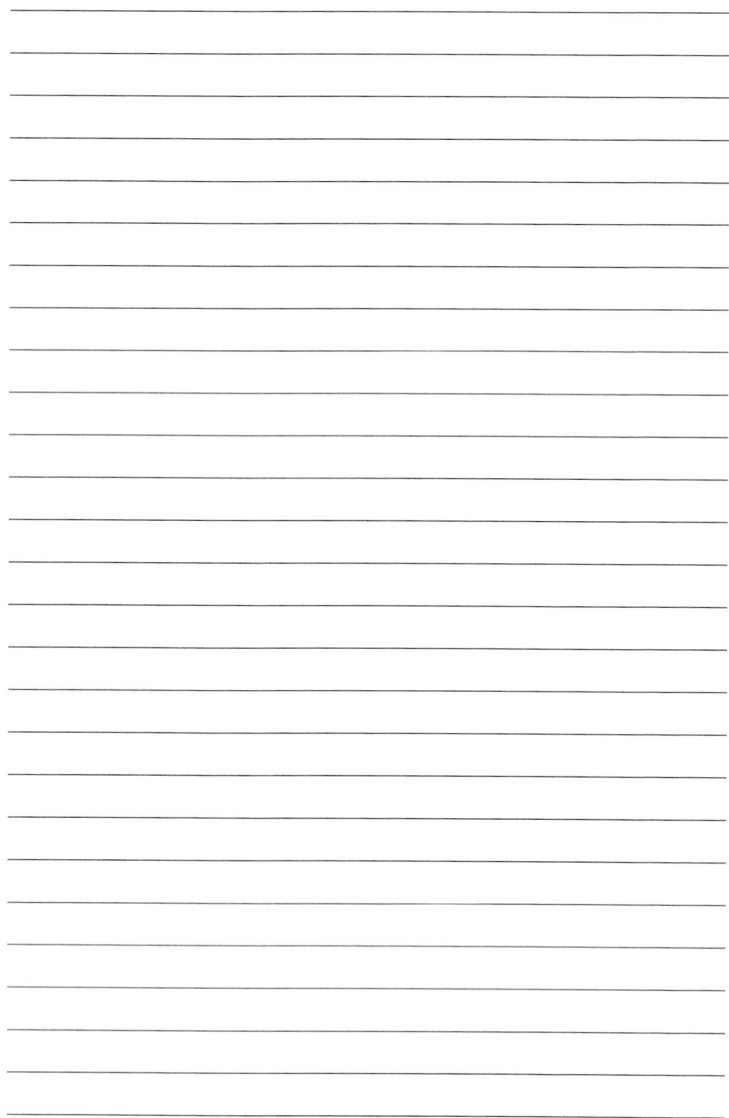

CHAPTER 13

WEAKENING THE STORM

A HURRICANE LOSES ITS STRENGTH AS IT TRAVELS OVER COOLER water. The cooler water prevents the hurricane from creating a continual supply of warm, moist tropical air which it needs to sustain itself. Just like the cool water, our Savior, Jesus Christ, can help us stop feeding our storms. But we need to be willing to move toward Him.

As you know by now, my trust in God's kindness, love, and support was very small. It hardly existed at all, but I knew that needed to change if there was going to be any chance of escaping this storm. Once again I turned to the scriptures to find Christ's characteristics. Here is a list of a few words that describe Him:

- Savior
- Breaks the bands of death
- Loosens chains
- Deliverer

- Invites to partake of happiness
- Arms are always open
- Continually ready to receive you
- Encouraging
- Supportive
- Watches over and protects
- Frees and liberates
- Patient
- Forgiving
- Everlasting love

My counselor shared with me an example of how we grow in faith. He drew a picture of an altar with four supporting legs. The altar represents the altar that we are upon, which we must eventually place our individual will. Each leg supports one corner of the altar and represents a stage of growth, or level of understanding in a person's faith. Accepting the first leg is necessary before the second leg can be accepted, and the second accepted before the third can be, and so forth. The first leg represents accepting that God exists. If we can't accept the existence of God then there is no use for the other three legs or the altar. If we can accept His existence then the next leg follows logically. The next leg represents understanding the nature of God—that He is all powerful, all knowing, and all loving. The third leg is that because God exists and is all powerful and all loving that we can trust that God knows, loves, and cares about each of us individually. Finally, if we have faith in the first three legs of the altar then we can accept the fourth leg, which represents understanding and accepting that God will never stop us from progressing, nor will He ever give us anything in our life that is meant to make us fail, nor anything that is designed to not help us progress toward becoming more like Him and returning to Him. No matter what happens in life, we have our agency and He is cheering us on. He wants us to come back home to Him. After my counselor showed me the four legs of the altar, he explained that once all four legs are accepted, strong, and steady, we can trust that God will direct our lives for our best good, even though it doesn't always seem that way in the moment, and thus we can prepare ourselves to opt into God's will. We are ready to lay it all on the altar and trust that in so doing we are doing what's best for us and those we love. (The concept of The Four Pillars of the Laying Your Will on the Altar of God is copyrighted © 2014 by Klayne Rasmussen, Ph.D., used with permission.)

I will admit that as I listened to my counselor's comparison of faith, studied the scriptures and highlighted the verses that define Christ's love, I felt a spark of remembrance, but doubt quickly smothered it. If I was to truly trust God again, I needed to know that He really knew *me* and loved *me* individually. I knew He existed and I knew He could do all things, but I didn't know of His love for me personally. It was easy for me to believe He loved and cherished everyone else, but I couldn't wrap my mind around why He would love me.

I had heard a suggestion once of writing a letter to God and then waiting for the response. I decided to try this one day and it turned out to be one of the most spiritual experiences I had had in a very long time.

Challenge: It's time to write a letter to God. I'm serious. I know you may be thinking, "He already knows what I'm thinking and feeling," but that doesn't matter. The purpose is to remind you of what you are thinking and feeling. If you don't quite know how to put it in words, review the brainstorming challenges given earlier in this book.

Here's what you do:

1: Say a quick prayer for protection from the adversary.

2: Get a blank piece of paper.

3: Write the date at the top and begin with, "Dear God,"

4: Begin to write everything you want to say to Him. Don't hold back if you are angry like I was. Write whatever comes to your mind. Tell Him about your frustrations, sadness, and lack of worth, trials, anger, whatever you are experiencing at this time. Don't edit; just write.

When you are finished, turn the page over or get a new one (if you used up both sides) and do the same thing by putting the date at top, but this time, start the letter with, "Dear (your name here),". Put your pen or pencil on the page and wait silently. Words and phrases will begin to come. Write them as they are! No editing! You will feel like what you are writing can't be true, but it is. God knows you better than you know yourself. Trust Him. C.S. Lewis puts it this way, "The more we let God take us over, the more truly ourselves we become—because He made us. He invented us. He invented all the different people that you and I were intended to be…It is when I turn to Christ, when I give up myself to His personality that I first begin to have a real personality of my own." (C.S. Lewis, **Mere Christianity**)

I know this challenge may be scary, but please trust God. He is a God of love and peace. He is the good Shepherd. He is anxiously awaiting your invitation to share His love with you. He wants you to see who you really are and everything that is good about you. God is a God of truth and His words are always full of light. He will not say anything that is intended to destroy or harm and if you start feeling this way, stop, pray for protection, and begin again. As you see yourself through God's eyes, you will begin to respect yourself so much more.

After you have completed both letters, every night before you go to sleep, read your letter from God. Reading this letter at the end of the day will remind you that no matter what happened or may happen tomorrow, you are loved, accepted, cherished, and of great worth from the One who matters most! Even if you don't believe what you are reading, read it anyway, every night, and soon you will begin to see the truth in the words that have been written.

I have completed this challenge: (date and sign)

_____

CHAPTER 14

EFFECTIVELY INTERRUPTING THE STRENGTH OF YOUR STORM

November 11, 2015 (AM)

*S*o, I *LISTENED AGAIN TO THE FIRST PART OF* KIRK DUNCAN'S CD, *"The Power of Forgiveness." After I did this, I knew what I had to do. I got on my knees and poured out my soul to God. I asked Him to forgive me for my stubbornness, pride, fear, lack of trust, lack of faith and hope and happiness, my anger, orneriness, resentment, frustration, lack of compassion, judgmental attitude, my need to please others before God, my worldliness, weariness, exhaustion, listening more to the "other" voices (Satan and his army), my lack of motivation and drive – especially in regard to gospel things like scriptures, prayer, and church attendance. I asked that he "take" from me my false comfort of darkness and anger, to release me from the illness and injuries I have been* *dealing with, and to help me have courage, trust, and faith. I also asked that he take away my loneliness.*

I visualized scooping all this darkness and goo out of me and placing it into a box (there was too much to hold in my hands). I then gave the box to God with a very heavy heart. I was embarrassed and sad to ask Him to take it from me. However, He did it without hesitation and it immediately disappeared. I would like to say that I feel lighter and happier. I do feel lighter in a way, but I mainly feel tired and like a void is inside me.

I thanked the Lord for His help and unconditional love. I asked that He help me remember this love so that I can stop listening to the "other" voices that constantly are trying to keep me from Him.

I don't know what my part is right now in His great plan, but I pray I will have the courage and strength to keep listening to the "good" voices and that soon I will know what my part is and where I am needed most right now in my life.

Forgiveness is a huge part of sucking the strength out of your storm. For me personally, I felt I had already forgiven who I needed to forgive and if I hadn't forgiven them, it was because they didn't deserve forgiveness or I couldn't bring myself to do it because I was still so angry and hurt. However, I knew deep down inside my heart that in order to be healed completely, I was going to have to let the anger and hurt go. So I took it upon myself to begin forgiving everyone I still felt I needed to forgive. This process wasn't easy and it didn't happen overnight.

March 8, 2016

I finally did it. I worked on forgiving today. I forgave, and forgave, and forgave. I know it sounds crazy, but I knew I needed to release past anger, frustration, disappointment, resentment, and hurt before I could move forward. As I began this process, I thought of each person I needed to forgive individually. This experience was a lot more difficult than I expected. I knew it was going to be hard because my anger and resentment had become a false sense of security to me. I figured if I stayed mad, I wouldn't be able to be hurt again. Obviously, this was just another way of destroying my happiness and worth.

What I didn't count on was the feelings of me having to be forgiven! Each time I thought of an individual and forgave them, I saw possible reasons for their actions (such as their home life, problems they were facing, their own insecurities, etc.) and realized I had been judgmental and prideful. Wow! I discovered I am very prideful and think I know better than everyone. What?! Oh yeah! That's the reality I was hit with today. That's what made this exercise even more painful.

As I forgave each person I envisioned, I asked them to please forgive me. This experience was exhausting, but also surprisingly lightening. I felt such a huge sense of relief! I'm sure there are more people to forgive and ask forgiveness of, but the first layer of the onion has been removed. And just like an onion, it brought a lot of tears, but the freedom was worth it all. How incredibly grateful I am for forgiveness.

Gordon B. Hinckley stated the following, "The willingness to forgive is a sign of spiritual and emotional maturity. It is one of the great virtues to which we all should aspire. Imagine a world filled with individuals willing both to apologize and to accept an apology. Is there any problem that could not be solved among people who possessed the humility and largeness of spirit and soul to do either—or both—when needed?" (Gordon B. Hinckley, *Standing for*

Something: 10 Neglected Virtues That Will Heal Our Hearts and Homes)

I continued to work on forgiveness, but it wasn't until about a month ago that I realized I had forgotten one very important person to forgive: *me*. This was the toughest person to forgive of all. I needed to forgive myself not only for all the negative emotions I had harbored for so long and the anger and resentment I had felt toward God, but I had to forgive myself for having depression in the first place. I had to let go of the feeling that being diagnosed with this illness was my fault because I was weak. I had to forgive myself for not being perfect and flawless. I had to forgive myself for all the unkind words, thoughts, and behaviors I directed toward myself. I had a lot to forgive and I knew it was an extremely important next step. C.S. Lewis said this, "To be a Christian means to forgive the inexcusable because God has forgiven the inexcusable in you." (C.S. Lewis, *The Weight of Glory*)

So, what gives you the right to not forgive yourself?

Forgiveness is an incredible gift that God has given us. He loves us so much and He understands the freedom forgiveness provides. Sometimes it's an easy process and sometimes it is incredibly difficult. Be patient with yourself as you work on forgiving.

Challenge: Make a list of all the people you feel you need to forgive on a separate piece of paper. Be sure to include yourself on that list. Go to God in prayer and ask for His help in forgiving. Ask Him to free you from past hurts so you can move forward into His light. Ask Him to help you break free of your storm and thank Him for the lessons you have learned from these past experiences. Don't worry if it takes time. God is focusing on your willingness to change for the better, not the speed in which it happens. Record your experiences below. By the way, be sure to rip up the paper with the names of those you need to forgive. No need to start up another storm.

_____

_____

_____

_____

_____

_____

_____

_____

_____

_____

_____

_____

_____

_____

_____

_____

_____

_____

_____

_____

_____

_____

CHAPTER 15

THE DISPERSING STORM

A S A HURRICANE LOSES ITS STRENGTH AND BECOMES DISORGA-nized, it no longer remains a hurricane. The storm system begins to break down and it slowly becomes a less threatening storm.

During the process of escaping your storm, it can be very tiring and at times discouraging. You may feel that all this work is getting you nowhere nearer to peace or happiness. You get tired of the continual ups and downs and can't see any end in sight. However, never forget, "The great thing to remember is that though our feelings come and go, God's love for us does not." (C.S. Lewis, *Mere Christianity*). And just like a hurricane that begins to disperse, there is hope of a clear sky.

At this particular time of my personal storm I became discouraged. I began worrying that holding on to hope was a mistake because my storm didn't show any indication of losing its strength. You see, it's not very easy to recognize when your storm is about to disperse because it is so consuming. One day I decided to focus my scripture study on hope. I read every scripture that applied and many articles as well. I knew I needed to hold on, that this storm would eventually pass, but I was tired of waiting and needed desperate help in acquiring hope.

I pondered and prayed over the topic of hope for about an hour. As I did, I began to understand what I needed to do to have hope in my life. Just like I had an evidence notebook to prove to myself that Satan was real and trying to bring me down through negative thoughts about myself, I needed to have my own evidence that God loved me and was showing me that love every day. I had the letter from God that expressed His love for me, but I needed visual evidence. If I could see God's hand, I would have the strength to keep holding on because I would know that He did care and was cheering me on daily. One of my favorite scriptures is Isaiah 41:13, "For I the Lord thy God will hold thy right hand, saying unto thee, *fear not*; I will help thee" (emphasis added).

Without hesitation, I went into my kitchen and pulled everything off of the magnet board hanging on the wall by our phone. I grabbed a blank piece of paper and wrote at the top; "What Wonders and Miracles Did You See Today?" in big, bold letters. I then printed the following scripture and hung it off to the side, "Eye hath not seen, nor ear heard, neither have entered into the heart of man, the things which God hath prepared for them that love him" (1Corintians 2:9). My goal was to write every single thing I saw that proved God was there and loved me.

Each day, I recorded what had made me happy or reminded me that I was loved on this magnet board. I placed colored markers next to it so I had fun colors to choose from. As I made a habit of looking at everything as a gift from God, my heart swelled with love and happiness. My self-worth increased because I realized I meant something to Him. The book, *A Simple Path*, attributes the following quote to Mother Teresa,

"God made the world for the delight of human beings — if only we could see His goodness everywhere, His concern for us, His awareness of our needs: the phone call we've waited for, the ride we are offered, the letter in the mail; just the little things He does for us throughout the day . As we remember and notice His love for us, we just begin to fall in love with Him because He is so busy with us — you just can't resist Him. I believe there's no such thing as luck in life, it's God's love." (Lucinda Vardey, *A Simple Path*)

I couldn't agree more. I wrote about the beautiful sunshine, the birds in the morning, my cute neighbors' kids bringing me cookies and making me smile, the unexpected phone call from a friend, and the great opportunities and people that came into my life. I was amazed that as time went by, I was writing more and more on my "Wonders and Miracles" board every day. It wasn't because God was blessing me any more than usual; it was because I had opened my eyes to see all the wonders around me.

Challenge: Make your own "Wonders and Miracles" board. Put this board somewhere you will see it daily. Make sure you add to it every day. If you see something or experience something wonderful while you are away from home, record it in your phone or on a piece of paper and add it to your board when you get a chance. Don't let any of these wonders and miracles you witness be forgotten! Remember, "Happiness isn't something that depends on our surroundings…it's something we make inside ourselves"(Corrie Ten Boom, *The Hiding Place*). The more we focus on God's love for us and the amazing ways He shows us daily, the easier it is to create that happiness within ourselves. List below where you are going to place your "Wonders and Miracles" board. If you don't have a board, just hang a blank piece of paper on your wall. Commit today when you will have it ready and commit to writing at least three things every day. Write, sign, and date your commitment below:

_____

_____

_____

_____

_____

_____

_____

_____

_____

_____

_____

_____

_____

CHAPTER 16

SET FREE

WHEN I WAS YOUNG, I MADE A PROMISE TO MYSELF THAT I would never stop praying. Even during the times of my life where I was angry with God, I prayed. I didn't put any heart or soul into it, but I did the actions. Some may feel that if you don't pray with a sincere heart, you shouldn't bother at all. I disagree wholeheartedly. I credit my actions of praying daily to my eventual escape. If I had closed off my communication with God entirely by not going through the motions of prayer, I would not have been able to hear His answers or feel His love when I was finally ready to receive them. I compare this experience to making a phone call or sending a text message. You may call or send a text to someone you really want to get a hold of, to which there is no response. You could choose to give up and turn your phone off altogether. However, if you leave your phone on you will get the response when it does come because you are doing your part to receive it. Think about it, how are you ever going to hear or feel anything God wants to tell you if you give up trying to listen to Him? As hard as it is sometimes, we need to remember that our answers aren't only dependant on God's timing, but on our willingness to listen and then act. I know I wasn't ready for a long time, but I kept "dialing" just in case.

Isaiah 1:18 reads, "Come now, and let us reason together, saith the Lord: though your sins be as scarlet, they shall be as white as snow; though they be red like crimson, they shall be as wool."

This scripture reminds us that God wants us to "reason" or brainstorm or discuss things with Him.

One of the more freeing experiences I've had was during the years I was incredibly angry with God. I was visiting with one of my counselors at the time and he asked me if I had expressed to God my anger, frustration, disappointment, resentment, lack of trust, and the feelings I had in regard to my situation being unfair. I remember looking at him and saying, "No way! I would totally get struck by lightning!" He then asked if I thought God wasn't aware of it already. Of course I knew He was, but I wasn't going to vocalize it to him! Was my counselor crazy? My language alone would be unacceptable in a prayer setting! My counselor continued to encourage me to voice my feelings to God, but I brushed it off.

A few days later, I experienced intense anger once again and decided I would take my chances and have it out with God. So what if I died from a lightning strike? At least this nightmare would be over. I began to explain (in not such nice words) my anger and frustration, my hatred and disappointment, my fears and feelings of abandonment. I sobbed as I expressed these feeling out loud to God. When I finished ranting, instead of lightning, I actually felt my

Savior put His arms around me. I felt my head resting on His lap. I felt His heart breaking because mine was so broken and hurt. At that moment, my relationship with God changed. God went from being my enemy to my greatest cheerleader, and the healing began.

As I write this and remember the tenderness of that experience, I am being taught. This was a great victory for me! You will begin to see that with every victory, Christ is by your side. He makes victories possible through His atonement and the compassion, empathy, and understanding He gained while in the Garden of Gethsemane.

If you feel abandoned, whatever you do, don't stop praying! If you already have, start today! You may feel you are talking to a wall; I did. But someday, because you are continuing to reach out to Him, you will hear and feel Him. He is there! God never, ever turns His back on us. It is us that turn our backs to Him. Show Him that you are still trying and you will never give up. Pray every morning and evening. Prove to Him and yourself that you are hopeful and looking for your escape. Make prayer your "steering wheel and not your spare tire" (Corrie Ten Boom, *Don't Wrestle, Just Nestle*), and remember, "In darkness God's truth shines most clear" (Corrie Ten Boom, *The Hiding Place*). Keep looking for it! Keep "dialing"!

Challenge: Make a plan to 'reason together' with God. List below the things you want to say to Him. Don't hesitate to write anything and everything you feel and want to express. The more honest and open you are, the sooner you will feel the closeness of God.

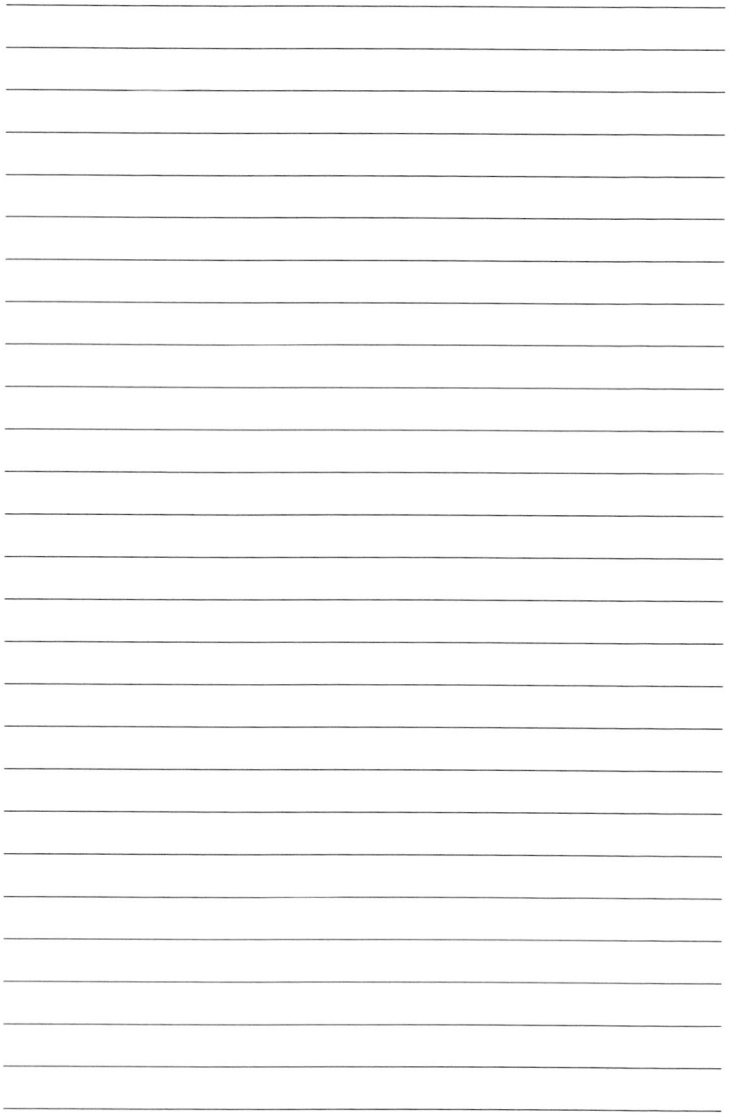

CHAPTER 17

HUMANITARIAN AID

AFTER EVERY STORM, THOUSANDS OF PEOPLE UNITE TO PROVIDE aid for the survivors. These individuals help with comfort, shelters, food, support, encouragement, and many more vital necessities. We too have humanitarian aid during our storms. Some of these individuals are a part of our everyday lives. For me personally, my humanitarian aid included my husband, children, parents, in-laws, friends, church leaders, and my counselors. But did you know that our personal humanitarian aid extends far beyond what we see?

One of my all-time favorite events in the Bible is found in 2 Kings chapter 6. The king of Syria is waging war on the Israelites. He sends spies to find out where Elisha and his army are so he can sneak in and destroy them. The spy returns and reveals the location of Elisha. That night, the army of the king sets forth and encircles Elisha's camp. Early the next morning, one of the servants of Elisha rises early and discovers the dangerous situation they are in. I am certain that he was terrified as he looked upon the innumerable hosts of the enemy's army that surrounded them with their horses and chariots. I can only imagine the amount of dread that must have filled his heart and soul at the sight. He runs to Elisha and asks, "Alas, my master! How shall we do?" In other words, what are we going to do? We are surrounded and our numbers are not as great. We are doomed! At this point Elisha says the following, "Fear not; for they that be with us are more than they that be with them." He then prays and asks the Lord to open the eyes of this servant to be able to see what he sees. Verse seventeen concludes with, "and, behold, the mountain was full of horses and chariots of fire round about Elisha."

We too have a portion of the hosts of heaven with us every single day! We also face a battle of innumerable forces in our world, but we have innumerable unseen forces round about us. We are never alone! Just as real as Satan and his army are, so is the army of God! We are surrounded by heavenly angels as well as earthly angels. Some of these heavenly angels are deceased relatives, friends, and even future posterity. Why would these heavenly beings not be cheering you on and helping you in your journey? Think about it, they love you so much! They want you to succeed. They recognize that if you give up or get lost in your storm, it could potentially harm or prevent your future children or grandchildren from being successful or existing at all. This is what Satan wants. Your guardian angels— or help on the other side, whatever you want to call them— are just waiting for you to invite them to join your battle with the adversary and help you in escaping your storm.

Not only are those on earth and those with God your humanitarian aid team, but so are *you*! *You* need to choose to never give up. No one can force you to do anything, especially God. I know it's hard. I know it's scary. I know it's exhausting. I know you feel broken and hopeless of ever feeling whole again. But if I can choose to fight, look to Christ as a friend and help, and escape my storm, so can you! Choose to keep going. Choose to try the best you can. God looks on the heart, not the amount accomplished. Choose to always *desire* happiness, hope, and self-worth. Remember this, "It is not so much the major events as the small day-to-day decisions that map the course of our living . . . Our lives are, in reality, the sum total of our seemingly unimportant decisions and of our capacity to live by those decisions" (Gordon B. Hinckley, *Caesar, Circus, or Christ?* Brigham Young University Speeches of the Year, 26 Oct. 1965, 3). God knows you, He trusts you. You are His and He loves you unconditionally. Choose to fight. Choose escape. Choose freedom!

Challenge: Commit today to never give up. Write your commitment, date it, and sign it. Next, make a list of your earthly angels and the heavenly angels you feel may be encircling you. You don't have to be right or one hundred percent certain. Pray first and then write the names that come to your mind. This exercise is to help open your mind to the possibilities of who God has helping you here on earth and on the other side.

_____

_____

_____

_____

_____

_____

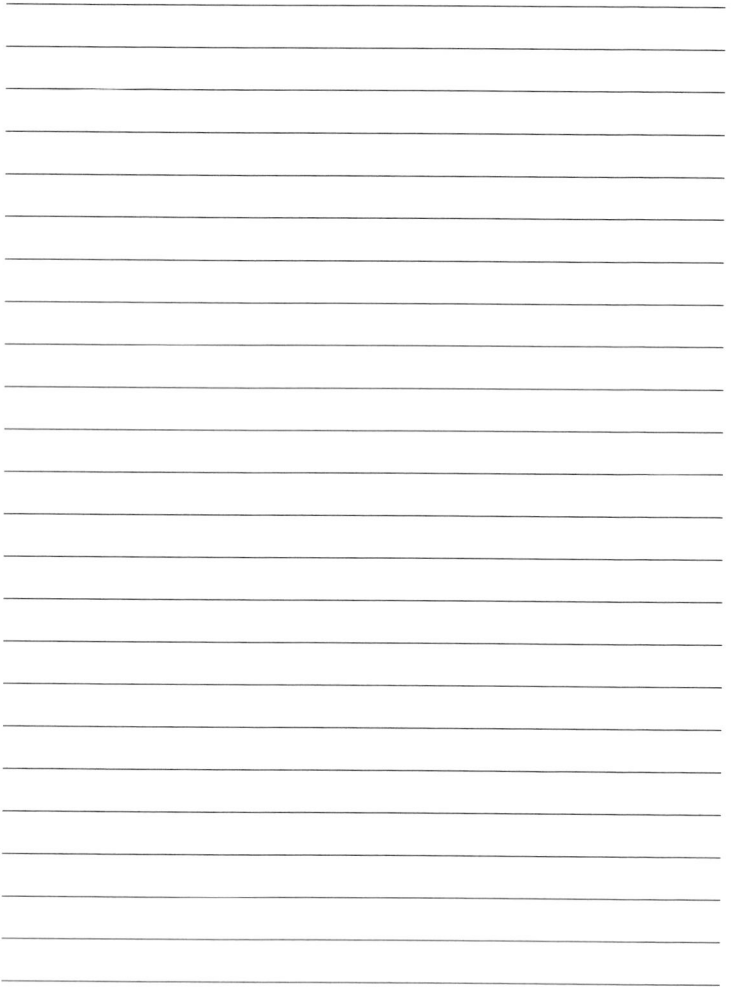

CHAPTER 18

SURVEYING THE AFTERMATH

A FTER A HURRICANE HAS PASSED, THE SURVIVORS EMERGE AND survey the aftermath of the storm. So many times over the past sixteen years I asked, "Why?" I couldn't understand why I had to endure something so awful for so long. Several times during my storm, I would survey the damage and be hit with discouragement as I saw the broken, weak, and fearful person I had become. Looking at the destruction before my storm had passed was not fair to me. Of course, there is much damage in the process of a storm! The true aftermath didn't manifest itself until after my escape.

I mentioned earlier in the chapter on forgiveness that I had to forgive myself for having depression. An exercise I did to help me do this involved writing all the emotions I experienced from the day I was diagnosed to the present day. I want to share with you some of that list to help you understand some of the "aftermath" of my storm.

During the Storm	Today
Betrayed	Guided
Abandoned	Supported
Unsupported	Encircled
Mocked	Stronger than ever
Confused	Excited
Angry	Enlightened
Darkness	Awakened
Burden	Set Free
Useless	Light
Hurt	Hopeful
Guilt	Loved and love others
Sorrow	Revived
Worthlessness	New life
Trapped	Self-worth
Afraid	Peace

The difference is amazing! During my storm all I could see was what was around me—all the hurt, darkness, sadness, and despair. Now that the storm has passed, I continue to see what is around me and have a greater appreciation for all of it. How often we take happiness for granted! My point in sharing this list with you is to show you the storm does end! Stop asking "why" and hold on to the fact that someday you will understand.

Right after making the above list I had the following experience. I wasn't intending on putting it in this book because it is very sacred to me so, I ask that you be respectful of the words you are about to read.

June 6, 2016 (AM)

God is good! I have been really struggling with the assignment I was given in regard to forgiving myself for having depression. The thought of reliving the pain and darkness was not at all something I wanted to do. All week I've been exhausted and avoiding it. Yesterday I fasted for help and this morning, I got it done.

I woke up extra early and poured out my heart to God. I expressed my fears and how overwhelmed I felt with this assignment. As I prayed, I felt impressed to just bullet-point the emotions so I wouldn't have to read though past journals. So I did.

Six pages later, my eyes were opened to how far I have come. I was intrigued by how God had taken the place of Satan in my mind early on. All the words I used to describe how I saw God were actually the characteristics of Satan. Wow!

As I was thinking about the huge change of heart, mind, and understanding I have experienced, I happened to see a quote posted on my emails that stated the following, "Everything you are going through is preparing you for what you asked for."

As I thought about this statement in regard to what I had just written and reflected on, I had a scene come to my mind of me planning my life on earth with God. He asked, "What do you want most to do on earth?" My response, "I want to be a messenger of Christ! But how am I going to remember Satan's true nature so as to teach and testify and bring others to you?" God responded, "You will experience depression."

Immediately I thought, "Wow! The chances God takes. I could have so easily continued down the path that separated me from Him." But just as quickly, the thought came, "Or is it that He trusts us?"

This has been such a sacred experience and as always, words cannot do it justice. I pray you will know the truth of it through the Spirit. This knowledge of the past sixteen years of depression changes everything! Do you see that? This has been an experience to remember. To prepare me to be a messenger of Christ! And what an amazing family I have for going through it with me!

One of my very favorite quotes in regard to trusting God is by C.S. Lewis. I have always loved it, but never thought I'd see the amazing "renovation" he talks of until now. He said,

"Imagine yourself as a living house. God comes in to rebuild that house. At first, perhaps, you can understand what He is doing. He is getting the drains right and stopping the leaks in the roof and so on; you knew that those jobs needed doing and so you are not surprised. But presently He starts knocking the house about in a way that hurts abominably and does not seem to make any sense. What on earth is He up to? The explanation is that He is building quite a different house from the one you thought of—throwing out a new wing here, putting on an extra floor there, running up towers, making courtyards. You thought you were being made into a decent little cottage: but He is building a palace. He intends to come and live in it Himself." (C.S. Lewis, *Mere Christianity*)

My escape from my storm was because I reached out to God for rescuing. It didn't happen as quickly as I would have liked. It was very hard to be patient and most of the time I wasn't, but God never gave up on me! Be patient with God and be patient with yourself. Be quick to forgive yourself and look at your mistakes as opportunities to learn. Corrie Ten Boom has said, "Never be afraid to trust an unknown future to a known God." (Corrie Ten Boom, *Clippings from My Notebook*) He has your back!

Challenge: What do you want most out of life? Do you see how your current situation may benefit you in achieving what you want most? If you are not there yet, that's okay. Start with making a list of how you currently feel and add to it as time goes on. Keep your mind open to seeing how each situation may lead to something incredible and good. Remember your "Wonders and Miracles" board. It will help in training your mind to see the good amidst the storm.

CHAPTER 19

EMBARK!

We're starting on a journey.
We're following the light.
It's giving us direction
Leading us through life.

We'll follow where it leads us
Wherever it may be
Whether to a land of promise
Or through the stormy seas.

No matter how far,
We're not afraid
His love will light the way.

So we will stand up
Altogether
Raise our eyes up
To the sky

With faith and love in our hearts,
We will EMBARK!

("Embark" by Elijah Thomas)

IN THE MERRIAM-WEBSTER DICTIONARY, EMBARK IS DEFINED AS "beginning a journey; to make a start; or to engage, enlist, or invest in an enterprise." When your storm has passed, it is your time to embark. It is time for you to begin a new journey, to start a new chapter in your life, and to continue to invest in your well-being and relationship with God.

The point of embarking is to look to the future. The glorious, marvelous, exciting future! Please understand that I am not encouraging you to focus on the future only. You need to enjoy the present — that's one of the reasons behind the "Wonders and Miracles" board. What I am proposing by inviting you to look to the future is to stop hanging out in the past. Be grateful for the memories and the lessons you have learned, but don't dwell on the sadness, disappointments, or the way you were hurt by others. It is over; you are stronger and ready to move forward! Remember, "We must be willing to get rid of the life we've planned, so as to have the life that is waiting for us" (Joseph Campbell, *A Joseph Campbell Companion: Reflections of the Art of Living*). The life we plan is nowhere near as great as the life God has in store for us if we are willing to take His hand and accept his help and guidance (see Isaiah 41:13).

Don't let fear hold you back. You and I have no idea the grand things that lie ahead for us. André Gide said this in regard to moving forward, "One does not discover new lands without consenting to lose sight of the shore for a very long time."(André Gide, *The Counterfeiters*) The thought of losing sight of the shore may feel scary, but switch that thinking to exciting! You have conquered your storm! You know how to conquer the next one and the one after that! You are empowered! God has a great mission for you! It is unique to you and you alone. You are needed. There are many in the world today facing their own storms. Take what you learn and share it with others. Help them escape and find Christ in the process. Remember, "Inasmuch as ye have done it unto one of the least of these my brethren, ye have done it unto me" (Matthew 25:40). What better way to show Christ your appreciation for helping you through your storm than by helping others through theirs?

God is a God of miracles. My life is one of those miracles. My escape from my storm of sixteen years is one of those miracles. There are miracles waiting for you. Don't give up. Keep going and those miracles will happen.

CHAPTER 20

WEATHER SATELLITES

O N June 19, 1999, NASA launched a spacecraft, Quick Scatterometer (QuickSCAT), with a device that uses a specialized microwave radar that measures near-surface wind speed and direction over the earth's oceans. Recently the ability to discover and track potential hurricanes has become possible due to weather satellites. This is a huge blessing because it not only allows for education on storm systems and how they develop, but it provides advanced warning to all who may be in its path.

We too have many "devices" to help in detecting potential storms, and although we may not be able to stop them from coming, we can protect ourselves from being destroyed. And sometimes we can avoid them all together! It's like having an evacuation plan!

As much as I would love to say that you are guaranteed to live happily ever after when your storm is gone, I can't. Life is meant to be a time to draw nearer to God and to discover who we really are. Often times, we are more receptive during difficult times. However, you are more powerful than you realize, and with every storm you encounter, you will discover more and more the true power you possess if you have God by your side. Yes, storms will happen, but now you know what to do to escape quickly and come out conqueror!

All the challenges in this book are your keys to freedom. Here is a brief reminder of each one:

1. Recognize the signs of an oncoming storm. (Chapter 2)

2. Be aware of your personal triggers. (Chapter 3)

3. Pinpoint the emotions forming your storm. (Chapter 4)

4. Be familiar with what emotions or situations are causing chain reactions. (Chapter 5)

5. Determine what is keeping your storm strong. (Chapter 6)

6. Seek help! Especially if you are thinking of suicide. (Chapter 7)

7. Contemplate why Satan wants you to be unhappy, in turmoil, and have a lack of self-worth. (Chapter 8)

8. Remember who you are fighting for. (Chapter 9)

9. Determine if you are really committed to breaking free. (Chapter 10)

10. Distinguish the ways Satan uses camouflage and the different traps he sets for you personally. (Chapter 11)

11. Continue to regularly use your Evidence Notebook. (Chapter 12)

12. Write another letter from God or continue reading the first one written. (Chapter 13)

13. Forgive, forgive, and forgive! (Chapter 14)

14. Continue using your "Wonders and Miracles" board. Every day be sure to list at least three evidences of God's love for you. (Chapter 15)

15. Keep praying! (Chapter 16)

16. Commit to never giving up. (Chapter 17)

17. Review and add to your list of earthly and heavenly angels. (Chapter 17)

18. Distinguish what it is you want most in life and then record in a journal or notebook how your storm is helping you achieve it. (Chapter 18)

19. Ask God to help you endure and have a desire for happiness, peace, hope, and self-worth (Chapters 16 and 18)

20. Embark on a journey of helping others. (Chapter 19)

21. Continually appreciate the present and look forward to the future with excitement. (Chapter 19)

22. Never forget that God loves you and has your back! (Chapter 19)

Refer to this list often and continue to explore and accept these challenges. As you do, these exercises will become second nature allowing you to be victorious in your battle for happiness and worth.

CONCLUSION

PEACE BE STILL

Master, the terror is over.

The elements sweetly rest.

Earth's sun in the calm lake is mirrored,

And heaven's within my breast.

Linger, O blessed Redeemer!

Leave me alone no more,

And with joy I shall make the blest harbor

And rest on the blissful shore.

(*Hymns.* "Master, the Tempest Is Raging," 105, vs. 3.
Words by Mary Ann Baker, music by H.R. Palmer)

September 15, 2016

W*ELL, I DID IT. I FINISHED WRITING THE BOOK GOD DIRECTED ME to write. I hope it helps others in their struggle for happiness and worth. If it benefits just one person, it will be worth it all. Not just the amount of time it took to write the book, but my whole sixteen year experience with depression.*

As I wrote about and relived those years, it was incredibly difficult. It brought back memories I didn't want to necessarily remember. I had many occasions where I felt under attack as I read journal entries about my inability to function and be there for my children. I used my evidence notebook a ton!

I also felt incredibly inept with the idea of writing this book. Not only was writing a book out of my comfort zone, but God kept changing everything in the process of my writing. My title changed, the direction I was heading changed, He asked me to put personal journal entries in it, and I knew he wanted it done by a certain date. Many days I let fear get in the way and I would hide instead of write.

One particular morning I was at my wits end. My gut was in knots and I feared letting my Savior down by not being able to do what He asked. As I prayed, these words came to my mind and I quickly wrote them down on the closest piece of paper I could find: God is a God of miracles and it's not just Him and me working on this book, it's tons of angels, God, and me! This is His will not mine alone. I am following His voice. This is what He wants…all I have to do is what He tells me to and He will do the rest with His team on the other side. I am not doing this alone! I am a small part of a huge plan. As long as I do my part, it will succeed and happen as God commands it to.

I am incredibly grateful for this experience. There were many times I cried as I wrote. Some tears were because of the sadness I once felt and some were because of the great goodness and love our Savior has for each one of us. There is no denying His hand in my life! I will forever give credit to Him for my escape and freedom.

I am on a new journey. I am embarking in the service of God and I am not alone in this endeavor. My ship is full of hope, happiness, excitement, earthly angels, guardian angels, and God. Storms may come, but I will never, never sink!

Everyone experiences storms, but we have a choice as to if we are going to remain in them forever, or set ourselves free with Christ's help. My prayer is that this journey through my personal storm has helped you discover how to escape from yours. I don't know you, but I love you nonetheless. You are always on my mind and I am praying for you every day. You may not feel it, know it, or understand it, but God loves you too! He loves you *everlastingly*! There is nothing you can do to stop His love for you. Keep fighting. You can do this. You are not alone! You are empowered and *will be victorious*!

ACKNOWLEDGEMENTS

I AM DEEPLY GRATEFUL FOR THE LOVE AND SUPPORT OF MY WONDER-ful husband and children these past sixteen years. I know I wasn't easy to live with, so thank you for never giving up on me and loving me unconditionally! I will forever be grateful for your many sacrifices in my behalf.

I am incredibly grateful to my counselors, especially Klayne Rasmussen, Ph.D., for his patience and encouragement through my extremely long learning process (I'm a bit stubborn). He taught me how to trust God again and didn't mince words when it came to what I needed to do. I will forever consider him an incredible gift and friend.

As I ponder on all who have helped me through my storm, I am deeply moved and humbled that so many stuck by my side. Thank you to my parents, in-laws, extended family, and friends. I couldn't have done it without you.

I would also like to express my gratitude for all who have been quoted in this book and have taught me so much in regard to mindset and God's everlasting love. I am grateful for my personal mentors, Kirk Duncan, Janette Van Leer, Tammy Ward, and Marnie Marcus. They are one of the main reasons this book is in your hands. I would also like to convey my sincere gratitude to my husband and the sweet friends that willingly read my rough drafts, edited, and honestly gave me feedback. I am also truly appreciative to my editor, KayLynn Flanders, my graphic designer, Angie at pro_ebookcovers on fiverr.com, and Createspace through Amazon. Without you, this book wouldn't have been possible. Thank you for your willingness to share your talents.

Finally, and most importantly, I would like to express my deep gratitude for my Heavenly Father and Savior, Jesus Christ. Thank you for rescuing me! Thank you for *always* having your arms open and loving me despite my anger. Thank you for your great sacrifice on my behalf and your endless patience and forgiveness. Thank you for making redemption possible. Thank you for holding my hand through the difficult process of reliving and sharing these dark times with the world. In short, thank you for *everything!*